MANAGEMENT

OF

COMMON

MEDICAL PROBLEMS

OF THE

ELDERLY IN PLAIN (NON-MEDICAL) LANGUAGE

E. GEORGE ELIAS, MD, PhD

BALBOA.
PRESS
A DIVISION OF HAY HOUSE

Balboa Press books may be ordered through booksellers or by contacting:

Balboa Press
A Division of Hay House
1663 Liberty Drive
Bloomington, IN 47403
www.balboapress.com
1 (877) 407-4847

Because of the dynamic nature of the Internet, any web addresses or
links contained in this book may have changed since publication and
may no longer be valid. The views expressed in this work are solely those
of the author and do not necessarily reflect the views of the publisher,
and the publisher hereby disclaims any responsibility for them.

The author of this book does not dispense medical advice or prescribe the use
of any technique as a form of treatment for physical, emotional, or medical
problems without the advice of a physician, either directly or indirectly. The
intent of the author is only to offer information of a general nature to help
you in your quest for emotional and spiritual well-being. In the event you use
any of the information in this book for yourself, which is your constitutional
right, the author and the publisher assume no responsibility for your actions.

Any people depicted in stock imagery provided by Getty Images are
models, and such images are being used for illustrative purposes only.
Certain stock imagery © Getty Images.

Print information available on the last page.

ISBN: 978-1-9822-2390-8 (sc)
ISBN: 978-1-9822-2389-2 (hc)
ISBN: 978-1-9822-2388-5 (e)

Library of Congress Control Number: 2019903206

Balboa Press rev. date: 03/18/2019

Contents

Glossaries

Medical terminology	Plain language explanation
Angina...............................	chest pain
Anticoagulant.....................	blood thinner
Antigens.............................	protein markers on cell surface & inside the cell
Atherosclerosis...................	hardening of arteries
Autoimmune Disease...........	person own immune system reject cells or organ in the body
BCG..................................	Bacillus Calmette Guerin
Blebs of emphysema............	air sacs in the lungs
COPD................................	chronic limitation of air flow from lungs
Cochlea..............................	structure in the inner ear
Coronary arteries................	arteries of the heart
Cystitis..............................	infected urinary bladder
Cytokine............................	hormones that activate some immune cells division
Disorder.............................	Disturbance in mental or health
Diverticulosis.....................	out pouching of the inner layer of the bowel through its wall

Introduction

It seems that people are living longer probably due to the medical research and its advances. Such long survival had resulted in more medical problems due to hidden genetic factors and the style of living. Such factors could have significant effect on how we age.

Common medical problems and some related conditions that affect the elderly are presented. These include elevated blood pressure (hypertension) and stroke, diseases of the blood vessels of the heart (coronary artery disease), angina (chest pain), loss of hearing, cancers, dementia including Alzheimer's disease, diabetes, arthritis, Parkinson's disease, cataract and loss of vision due to degenerating retinal cells (macular degeneration).

In addition, people over 65 years of age are liable to fall and sustain bone fracture most commonly of the hip, wrist and back. As we age, other symptoms can affect our overall health and the quality of life. These include slow reaction time, thinner skin that leads to tears and wounds that heal very slowly. In addition, weakness in the immune system can expose us to various infections and other diseases. Furthermore, loss of taste and smell can lead to loss of appetite and weight loss.

A large bulk of medical research refers to "The Stem Cell" which is the mother cell and the body's raw material from which all other specialized function body cells are generated such as heart cell, liver cell, brain cell and so on. This could get involved in the future repair of some damages caused by aging.

Medications in this publication are mentioned by their function only and not by their commercial or chemical name (to avoid any claims of commercial favoritism). The patient can ask the physician to which function does a given medication belong to. This allows a person to share the knowledge of his medical status.

Elevated Blood Pressure = Hypertension

t can occur in any age, including children, adolescence, adults and more commonly in the elderly for a variety of reasons. A blood pressure over 130/80 is considered an elevated pressure. Over 28% of the American population have elevated blood pressure with 3-18% are diagnosed annually depending on age, sex and body type. Unfortunately, the incidence is on the rise. The risk of developing hypertension includes kidney causes, general health, life style and family history.

The causative factors include: stress, lack of sleep, sleep apnea (interrupted breathing), too much salt or sugar in the food and thyroid conditions (producing high or low thyroid hormone), renal (kidney) and adrenal (a gland located above the kidney) causes may require surgical treatment. In addition, some of the over the counter medications, specifically non-salicylate pain medications, dehydration, air pollution, smoking and alcohol over consumption and old age can be the underlying factors.

The treatment consists of healthy diet and taking medications to lower an elevated blood pressure. **The diet:** includes fruit, vegetables, whole grain bread and keep the body weight down. Stop smoking and reduce alcohol consumption. **Medications:** are given by prescription and includes 1. Diuretics that increases urination and reduce the sodium and fluid in the body. 2. Drugs that help to relax the muscles of the blood vessels. 3. Medication that widen the blood vessels. 4. Medications that reduces the heart rate. 5. Medication that reduce the amount of calcium entering the heart. 6. Drugs that may prevent constriction of blood vessels. Each of these drugs has specific method of action and are used in combination. The untreated hypertension can cause major complications that includes; stroke, heart attack and loss of the extremity, specifically lower limb due to hardening of the arteries.

The management of hypertension requires the cooperation of the patient and the treating physician or nurse practitioner during the treatment and follow-up.

Coronary Artery Disease And Angina

t means disease that affect the vessels (arteries) that supply blood to the heart. It is caused by narrowing or blockage of the blood vessels of the heart by cholesterol and fat deposit followed by calcium deposit forming plaques inside such vessels and hardening of the vessels. This leads to narrowing, clogging or blockage of the vessels and depriving the heart muscle from blood flow and oxygenation.

Coronary artery disease is very common in the older population. It is characterized by tightness in the chest, chest pain (Angina Pectoris) that may travel to the shoulder, arm, back, neck or jaw. It may be accompanied by shortness of breath and fast heartbeat. The risk factors include persistent high blood pressure, high blood cholesterol, diabetes, smoking and possibly some genetic factors. The condition may lead to stable angina (chest pain with exercise or stress) with no pain at rest, while unstable angina (the pain is more severe and occur at rest). If not treated, it can lead to the death of part of heart muscle "myocardium" and the condition is called "myocardial infarction". On the other hand, a rare type of angina is called "Variant Angina" is caused by a temporary spasm in the coronary vessels without any dangerous effect.

Prevention: stop smoking, reduce stress, consult your physician on the use of low-dose aspirin as a blood thinner or similar agent to help blood flow through the vessels.

Diagnosis and Treatment:

1. Electrocardiogram (ECG) to show any changes which may be old or new.

2. Echocardiogram using sound wave to see if all parts of heart muscle are functioning (pumping) well.

3. Blood test to identify any elevation of heart muscle enzymes, which could indicate muscle distress. This may take 12 hours to rise after an attack.

4. Stress test with treadmill or nuclear stress test to measure blood flow to the heart muscle.

5. Cardiac catheterization and the injection of special dye to view the blood flow in the arteries of the heart. If any narrowing is noted, a balloon is introduced through the catheter and inflated to dilate the obstruction and result in better blood flow. A mesh tube called 'stent' can be inserted through the catheter into the dilated segment of the artery to maintain its patency.

6. Heart scanning which is performed by computerized tomography (CT) scan to identify the sites of calcium deposit in heart vessels.

In the meantime, the patient is placed on cholesterol reducing drugs, specifically the low-density lipoprotein (LDL) the bad cholesterol. The patient should be placed on some type of anticoagulant such as low-dose aspirin or similar agent, calcium channel blocker, nitroglycerin for any residual occasional chest pain, angiotensin-converting enzyme and angiotensin II receptor blocker to lower the blood pressure. Fish oil capsules which are rich in omega-3 and fish diet are highly recommended.

Finally, if symptoms persist, open heart surgery is considered to bypass blockage sites in the coronary arteries by using patients own veins.

Auricular Fibrillation

This is one of the most common heart problem in the elderly. It results when the upper two chambers of the heart (atria) do not work in coordination with the 2 lower heart chambers (ventricles).

The symptoms include heart palpitation (unusual heavy beating of heart) with irregular rhythm, shortness of breath, weakness and chest pain. Improper functioning of the heart can result from persistent high blood pressure, history of heart attack, diseases of heart blood vessels, abnormal heart valves, overactive thyroid gland, exposure to stimulant such as medication and tobacco, sleep disorder, lung disease, viral infections, obesity and alcohol consumption.

Treatment: aims to reset the heart rhythm to normal by anti-arrhythmic (against irregular rhythm/pulse) drugs, blood thinner to prevent clots, electrical cardioversion (using electrical shocks to the heart through electrodes placed on the chest), catheter ablation (by scarring and destroying tissues in the heart that triggers the abnormal heart beat) and radiofrequency ablation (in which part of the electrical conduction system of the heart is destroyed by heat generated from medium frequency alternating electric current generated by the radiofrequency).

Stroke = Cerebrovascular Disease

t is more common in elderly population, but it occurs at all ages. It affects 7.4 million patients and it is the 5th leading cause of death in USA with over 140,000 per year.

There are two types of strokes: 1. Ischemic; (no blood flow) which is the most common, and is caused by blockage of a blood vessel in the brain. 2. Hemorrhagic; (bleeding) caused by ruptured of an aneurysm or blood vessel in the brain. Both types deprive part of the brain of blood and oxygen, causing brain cells damage. Some people may experience temporary disruption of blood flow to the brain known as "Transient Ischemic Attack" (TIA) that does not cause permanent damage, but should be investigated to prevent future stroke.

Several conditions can lead to stroke and all deal with the conditions of the blood vessels. Narrowing of major blood vessels such as the carotid, vertebral arteries (both located in the neck) or intracranial (inside the skull) vessels or malformation in the vessels can be the underlying reasons. High blood pressure can cause changes in the blood vessels that result in narrowing of the blood vessels leading to ischemic changes in the brain, or rupture causing hemorrhagic stroke.

The best cure is by prevention. Control of the blood pressure is one the most important approaches. The early symptoms that justify medical intervention include sudden onset of dizziness, nausea, vomiting, headache, confusion, disorientation, memory loss, numbness, one sided arm or leg or face weakness, slurred speech and difficulty in comprehension. Late symptoms include one side paralysis, confusion, may be loss of half of the vision or loss of balance depending which part of the brain is affected.

The carotid arteries in the neck are to be evaluated by palpation to make sure that there is pulse without thrill and by stethoscope to listen to any thrill. Sonogram (sound wave) of the neck will identify any narrowing in the carotids. This is dealt with surgically to establish patency (being patent and opened). Additional radiological studies could identify similar problems at the vertebral and intracranial vessels. Any lesions (narrowing) that cannot be approached surgically can be treated with anticoagulant (blood thinner) and thrombolysis (dissolving the clots) drugs to establish patency of the vessels. In the meantime, physical therapy should be maintained to keep the muscle in fair shape until neurological recovery.

Loss of Hearing

N aturally, as humans age, different ailments tend to become a part of human life and one of them is hearing loss. Its onset can be sudden or gradual. It is one of the most common conditions that can affect the older population. Approximately, one in three people age 65-74 has hearing loss, and almost half of those older than 75 have difficulty hearing. According to the World Health Organization, 33% of global population above 65 year of age have disability hearing loss.

The causes vary and include: 1. Ear wax accumulation. 2. Damage to the inner ear by aging and/or exposure to loud noise that may cause wear and tear and damage to the hair cells (nerve cells) in the cochlea (in the inner ear) that send sound signals to the brain. 3. Heredity. 4. Drugs such as gentamycin and certain chemotherapy. 5. Some illnesses that cause high fever.

Treatment Options: 1. Ear wax removal with immediate improvement. 2. Damage to the inner ear has to be decided by a specialized Ear-Nose-Throat (ENT) doctor to rule out any tumor of the hearing (auditory) nerve. If the hearing loss is due to damage in the inner ear and is mild to moderate, a variety of hearing aids can be recommended by the Audiologist. Some of these devices are inserted in the ear, while other are applied behind the ear. These amplify the sounds and direct it into the ear. 3. However, if the hearing loss is severe or profound, Cochlear Implants are considered. It requires surgical intervention by inserting a microchip under the skin behind the ear with insertion of its probe into the cochlea.

Dementia

I t is the name of a group of brain disorders that affect memory, thinking, communication, and may be accompanied by anxiety, hallucination and mood swings. Alzheimer's disease is the most common disorder.

Types of Dementia

I. Vascular Dementia

It usually follows a stroke. It starts with memory loss, then trouble understanding, speaking, confusion, agitation, change in personality and mood, and problem in walking and having frequent falls.

II. Lewy Bodies Dementia

It is due to deposition of some type of protein in the brain causing some areas in the brain to become non-functional. The symptoms include problems in thinking, memory trouble, visual hallucination, sleepiness during the day, problem with movements, trembling, trouble walking and confused dreams.

III. Frontotemporal Dementia

Affect people between ages 45-60. These patients notice trouble in driving and cooking. The causes are unknown but it is due to the death of two parts of the brain (front and side). It affects the part of the brain that control social skills and decision making.

No special treatment for this rare group of disorders except for management of symptoms.

IV. Alzheimer's Disease

Alzheimer's disease is the most common cause of dementia. It is estimated that 5.7 million American are living with this disease, and such number is expected to rise. It is more prevalent in women than men. It is the 6th most common cause of death in USA. Between the years 2000 and 2015, the death rate from Alzheimer's rose 123%, with one in three seniors dying from this disease (more than breast and prostatic cancers combined).

Alzheimer's cannot be prevented, cured or slowed down. It places a huge burden on health care systems with an annual cost exceeding a quarter of a trillion dollars. Early diagnosis using a special imaging technique of the brain, and the development of biomarkers, helps in establishing the diagnosis in early stage and the initiation of early supportive therapy.

What is Alzheimer's Disease? It is the shrinking and atrophy (waist away) of the posterior part of the brain by the deposit of an abnormal protein known as Amyloid Plaques that destroys brain tissue. In addition, some brain cells die due to the presence of other abnormal proteins inside the cells. This will result in clinical symptoms that consist of a gradual decline in memory. These symptoms are divided into three stages: 1. Early stage that includes misplacing items, forgetting names, repeating same questions and hesitation. 2. Middle stage: confusion, disorientation, believing in things that are not true, impulsive behavior, problem talking and disturbed sleep. 3. Late stage:

difficulty moving around without help and gradual loss of speech.

At present, the management of the patient focusses on maintaining the mental function, managing the behavior symptoms and self-care. Medications include drugs that compensate for the death of some nerve cells in the brain. Futuristic approaches include two major therapeutic approaches; 1. anti-amyloid antibodies which showed promise in reducing the amount of amyloid in the brain with some clinical improvement. 2. Stem cell therapy which has not been tested in human, but in mice it showed some benefits in 2 approaches; the implantation of cells that develop to nerve cells or cells that produce a protein to support the growth and survival of nerve cells in the brain.

DIABETES

t is a general term referring to disorders characterized by excessive urine excretion. There are two main forms of this metabolic disorder that can lead to such a phenomenon: Diabetes Mellitus and Diabetes Insipidus. These two have no relation to one another. While diabetes mellitus is due to a lack of adequate type of insulin, diabetes insipidus is due to a lack of "antidiuretic hormone" (hormone that reduces frequency of urination) that is being secreted from the pituitary gland in the brain. The only common thing between the two diseases is frequent urination and thirst.

Diabetes Mellitus: is the most common metabolic disorder. It has three forms known as: Type I, Type II and Gestational. <u>Type I:</u> is more common in young individuals. It is an autoimmune disease (patients' own immune systems attack and reject own insulin producing cells in the pancreas). As a result, the body cells cannot utilize the glucose (sugar) due to inadequate or lack of insulin. This is treated by insulin injections with close monitoring of the patient. <u>Type II</u>, the pancreas continues to produce insulin but the body cannot make use of it. It is mostly common in old age population. This is managed by oral medications such as "Metformin" that improves insulin sensitivity and decreases intestinal absorption of glucose. <u>Gestational Diabetes</u> is a rare condition that occurs in pregnant women and should be treated aggressively with insulin injections to prevent problems to both the mother and the unborn child. It is a self-limiting disease that disappears after the child birth. However, the mother and child may develop type I diabetes later in their lives.

Diabetes Insipidus: It is the rarest form with only fewer than 20,000 patients diagnosed annually. It is caused by a deficiency of

Antidiuretic Hormone (ADH) which is secreted by the pituitary gland. The dysfunction of the pituitary gland by presence of a pituitary tumor, infection, genetic causes, kidney disease or induced by anti-viral drugs. The symptoms include frequent urination, thirst, fever and trouble sleeping. The treatment consists of adequate hydration, reduction of salt intake and treatment of the pituitary disorder by the administration of antidiuretic hormone.

Arthritis

t is a term describing pain in one or more joints. Such pain develops gradually or suddenly.

There are more than 100 different form of arthritis. While **osteoarthritis** is the most common type, **rheumatoid arthritis** comes second. Other types of arthritis could be due to infection or underlying systemic diseases such as lupus, gout, psoriasis, etc.

Osteoarthritis: It is a degenerative chronic condition that is the result of wear and tear in the joint that produces inflammation and destroys the cartilage within the joint. Osteoarthritis affects over 27 million Americans. It may be caused by an old injury and/or genetic factors. The symptoms include joint pain and stiffness, and is most common in the hands and fingers at the onset but can involve other joints later including knees, hips and spine. Morning stiffness is common and may last for 30 minutes. It is most prevalent in women, and has no other manifestations. It is a slow progressive disease. The diagnosis can be established by x-Ray and blood tests to rule out rheumatoid type.

Rheumatoid Arthritis: It is a complex autoimmune (patient own immunity) disease. Initially, the diagnosis could be confused with osteoarthritis. However, it differs in several ways: It causes inflammation in multiple joints throughout the body with systemic manifestation in the form of fatigue, fever, weight loss and loss of appetite. It affects 1.3 million people, mostly women. It is characterized by rapid onset and progression in people 30-60 years of age, but may develop in young age groups. These patients are also at risk of developing lupus and lymphomas (cancer in the lymph glands).

The treatment is mostly the same for both types of arthritis. On the other hand, the treatment of other forms of arthritis should be directed to management of the underlying disease such as lupus, gout and others.

The treatment aims to control pain, minimize joint damage and improve or maintain the quality of life. It involves medications, physical therapy and patient education and support. The medications: 1. Analgesics for pain control, but it has no effect on the inflammation. These include Tylenol and Percocet. 2. Anti-inflammatory drugs which reduces pain and inflammation. These include Motrin, Advil and Aleve. 3. Counterirritant: These contain menthol or capsaicin and are applied to the skin over the affected joint creating heat and modulate pain. 4. In osteoarthritis, if joint destruction is significant, partial or complete surgical replacement of the joint is indicated. 5. Antirheumatic drugs; to treat rheumatoid arthritis and stop the immune system of the patient from attacking the joint. These include biological agents such as Enbrel which was genetically engineered to target various protein molecules involved in immune response. 6. Cortisone that reduces inflammation and suppress the immune response.

Parkinson's disease

arkinson's disease is clinically characterized by tremors or shaking which usually begins in the hand and fingers, reduce ability to move and makes simple tasks difficult due to rigidity of the muscles and postural instability. It affects one million people in the USA and four million worldwide. About 60,000 are diagnosed every year in the United States with a peak incidence between ages 75-84. 86% have unknown reasons, and only 7% are induced by drugs. It is more common in men than women.

It is caused by low brain dopamine. It may result from: 1. Brain damage from anesthesia drugs. 2. Carbon monoxide exposure. 3. Some medications that are used to treat mental disorders. 4. Mercury poisoning. 5. Overdose of narcotics.

As of today, there is no cure for this disease. However, regular physical exercise, massage and healthy diet can help the patient initially by improving the symptoms, but such benefit frequently diminishes and becomes less consistent.

Several medications with a variety of actions have been established: 1. Drugs that can go to the brain and convert to dopamine. 2. Drugs that simulate dopamine i.e. mimic dopamine and affect the brain like dopamine, but do not convert to dopamine. 3. Drugs that inhibit breakdown of dopamine in the brain. 4. Drugs that prolong the effect of drugs # 1 by blocking the breakdown of dopamine. 5. Drugs that control tremors. 6. Drugs that give short relief of tremors. Each of those drugs has side effects and the treating physician should be informed by the patient or the family.

Surgical intervention may be needed. The neurosurgeon can implant electrodes into a special part of the brain, and connects them to a small generator which is implanted under the skin of the upper chest. Futuristic approach includes "Stem Cell Therapy" which is a research project that is attempting to develop cells that can produce dopamine to replace the dying dopamine cells in the brain.

Immunotherapy to Treat Cancer

mmunotherapy is the new and effective approach against some types of cancer. It is used in three different manners:1. Neoadjuvant therapy administered before surgical resection of the tumor to utilize the tumor markers (antigens) to induce anti-tumor specific immune response. 2. Adjuvant therapy administered after surgical excision of high risk tumors to prevent tumor recurrence and spread. 3. Therapeutic to treat recurrences and metastases. Furthermore, several types of immunotherapy are used to treat cancer. These include:

1. Check point inhibitors: are drugs that do not target the tumor directly, but interfere with the ability of certain protein molecules such as PD-1, PDL-1 and CTLA4 from protecting cancer cells from the immune surveillance. These drugs are approved for treatment of melanoma, some lung cancers, kidney and bladder cancers and head and neck cancer.

2. Adoptive cell transfer: is a treatment that attempts to boost the natural ability of the T cells (a type of white cell in the blood and are part of the immune system) to fight cancer. In such treatment, T cells are taken from the patient's own tumor and grown in large quantities in the lab then given back to the patient through his/ her vein. It is a long procedure for preparation and very expensive as it needs special sterile laboratories.

3. Monoclonal antibodies: are immune system proteins, created in the lab. These specifically attach themselves to the tumor cells but lack the ability to kill the tumor. Therefore, they are utilized as carriers of tumor-specific toxins.

4. Vaccines: Patient's own tumor cells are obtained from fresh resected tumors, cultivated in the lab, irradiated, mixed with material that activates the immune system called "adjuvant" and then reinjected in the skin of the patient. It is utilized to prevent recurrence of the tumor after surgical resection.

5. Cytokines: Two of them, namely interferons and interleukins are utilized in high-doses with major toxicity and minimal tumor shrinkage. However, when some other cytokines are given in small dosage at the tumor sites, they can induce a specific antitumor response to the patient own tumor in high risk melanoma and probably other cancers.

6. BCG: (Bacillus Calmette Guerin) when given in the urinary bladder through a catheter, it gives an excellent response to cancer of the urinary bladder, but only if the cancer is superficial (not invasive) in nature. On the other hand, when injected in melanoma of the skin, it gives good response but with major side effects.

7. Modified Polio Virus: The administration of modified polio virus in the tumor seems to show some benefits in the deadliest brain tumor known as "glioblastoma". Patients with such tumor have less than one year survival after surgery, chemotherapy and radiation therapy. It seems the administration of polio vaccine in such a tumor can result in shrinkage of the tumor and prolongation of patients' survival. This is under further investigation. Fighting cancer will continue through research.

What are the Stem Cells?

They are the mother cells and the body raw material from which all other cells with specialized function are generated under the right conditions in the body or in the laboratory. Stem cells can be cultured to form new stem cells or become specialized cells with certain function such as blood cells, brain cells, heart muscle or bone.

There are mainly two types of stem cells: 1. Embryonic stem cells, and 2. Adult stem cells. The <u>embryonic stem</u> cells are developed in the laboratory, from a fertilized egg. Over 3-5days, it will grow to an embryo of about 150 cells, all are stem cells. These can be cultured and divided into more stem cells or matured to become any type of cells in the body. They are being used in humans to treat macular degeneration which is a progressive blinding disease. However, this technique is facing some ethical concern as it sacrifices future embryo. On the other hand, <u>adult stem cells</u> are found in small number in the bone marrow and fat. These were thought to have limited ability to give rise to different cells in the body. However, new evidence revealed that bone marrow stem cells can give rise and mature to different types of cells. These are being tested in neurological and heart diseases. However, these cells are not as versatile and durable as embryonic stem cells.

Two additional experimental types are being investigated: 1. Genetic (hereditary) reprograming of regular adult fat cells into stem cells which can mature to heart cells in animal models. However, there is major concern about side effects. 2. The other one is Perinatal stem cells which are stem cells identified in the amniotic fluid (the sac around the fetus in the uterus during pregnancy) and also in the blood of the umbilical cord at time of delivery of the new born baby. These can develop into specialized cells, but these cells are not always available.

Researchers grow stem cells in the laboratory for two objectives: 1. It is to maintain the availability of stem cell lines for research. 2. These cells can be manipulated to specialize into specific types of cells such as heart muscle, nerve cells or blood cells. Theoretically and in futuristic approach, stem cells that are manipulated to become mature heart muscles could be injected into a patient after heart attack and could result in repairing the defect left in the heart.

Common Eye Diseases

There are four major age-related eye diseases: cataracts, glaucoma, diabetic retinopathy and macular degeneration.

I. Cataracts

It is <u>opacification (whitening) of the lens</u> of the eye. Among the causes are aging, family history, diabetes, excessive exposure to sunlight and previous eye surgery. The lens in the eye gets cloudy from clumping of the proteins within the lens. The patient complains of blurred vision, double vision, difficulty seeing at night, needs much bright light to read, seeing halos around the light, eye pain and/or headache. The disease is treated by surgical removal of the affected lens and replacing it with a plastic one.

II. Glaucoma

It is due to the <u>"increased pressure in the eye"</u>. There are no symptoms at the onset of the disease. However, with disease progression there could be occasional pain, blurred vision, narrowed and tunnel vision. As the disease progresses, there will be loss of peripheral vision, seeing halos around the lights, redness in the eye followed by loss of vision. Medical treatment should be tried first and it includes the following: medications that reduce production of eye fluid, drugs to help the outflow of the fluid from the eye, drugs to stimulate certain receptors and others to reduce eye pressure. Laser surgery is the last option with continuation of medications (if so needed).

III. Diabetic Retinopathy

This disease is the leading cause of blindness. Patients with uncontrolled diabetes can have "damage of the blood vessels in the retina", at the back of the eye, and these are replaced by new blood vessels that leak. The symptoms include retinal swelling, blurriness, loss of central vision, black spots in the field of vision, difficulty in perceiving colors then blindness. Treatment: for mild to moderate disease, close observation and control of diabetes. In severe cases, the use of drugs that prevent the growth of new vessels and cortisone injections in the eye to reduce the swelling in the retina.

IV. Macular Degeneration

Macular degeneration is a progressive vision impairment disease that results from "degeneration of the cells at central part of the retina", known as 'the Macula". This results in blurred vision and change in color perception. It is common in the elderly population.

The exact cause is unknown. However, some risk factors that predispose to the disease include aging, family history, smoking and race as the disease is more common in Caucasians. At present the treatment aims to slow down the progression of the disease and prevent vision loss.

There are two types of macular degeneration: The dry and the wet one. The dry macular degeneration is the most common. It usually starts in one eye then affects both. It does not affect the peripheral part of the retina and therefore it does not progress to total blindness. However, it can progress to wet type characterized by the development of new blood vessels under the retina that may leak. The wet macular degeneration can cause acute onset with sudden changes in vision.

Prevention: routine eye examinations, management of other coexisting medical problems, avoiding or quitting smoking and eating a diet rich in fruit, vegetables and fish (rich in omega-3 fatty acids). The recommended treatments include vitamin A supplement, anti-angiogenesis drugs that prevent vessel formation in wet types, laser therapy, photodynamic (light) therapy and low vision rehab. A new approach that is on clinical trials in few special medical center is the transplantation of embryonic stem cells with very successful outcome.

Respiratory
Disorders

I n addition to lung cancer, significant other respiratory diseases do occur in the elderly and include: pneumonia, asthma, emphysema, mesothelioma, pulmonary embolism, pulmonary hypertension and idiopathic pulmonary fibrosis.

I. Pneumonia

Pneumonia is an infectious disease of the lung and it ranges from mild to severe with fatal outcome. While elderly people can get pneumonia from close contact with other infected patients, yet the main way to get pneumonia is from themselves. To explain this, everybody carries bacteria in their noses and throat, and older, weak people cannot clear these secretions. Therefore, such secretions can go down into the lung and fill the airway with mucus, then pus, which interferes with breathing and deprives the body of oxygen. The bacterial infection can reach the blood stream causing sepsis.

Elderly people are more frail and they cannot clear their lungs' secretions by deep breathing and coughing to avoid infection. In addition, they have weak immune system and have a hard time fighting infection. They may also have other ailments such as diabetes and heart disease that put them at higher risk. Some lung conditions may also increase the risk such as chronic bronchitis, chronic obstructive pulmonary disease (COPD), asthma and emphysema.

Prevention can play a major role in this disease. Stop smoking. Correct abnormal breathing such as sleep apnea. Flu shots once a year, pneumonia vaccine against streptococcus pneumonia as one shot for life time. Use humidifiers to loosen up mucus and make it easy on the person to cough it out.

The patient usually presents with one or more of these symptoms: cough, fever, chills, shortness of breath, chest pain, sputum (yellow, green or bloody), and the patient may feel weak and may become confused from brain anoxia (low oxygen). The diagnosis can be established by physical examination confirmed by chest x-ray and supported by blood test.

Treatment: Rest, use of humidifiers and antibiotics. Encourage deep breath and cough or airway suctioning. Use of medication to make the patient cough or suppress the dry cough. Mild cases can be treated at home, however severe cases require hospitalization. People with pneumonia or recovering from pneumonia should have breathing tests and check oxygen level in the blood.

II. Asthma

It affects all ages and is common in the elderly. It is a chronic inflammatory lung disease. The exact cause is unknown but it could be due to genetic or environmental causes with high response of the airway to various stimulants such as exposure to dry dust, animal dander or pollens. The symptoms include labored breathing, audible wheezing, short breath, low blood pressure and low oxygen saturation below 90%. Treatment: the use of nasal oxygen, inhalers to dilate the airway, steroid therapy by inhalers and orally.

III. Emphysema

It is an over expansion of the terminal bronchi (air tubes) and lung alveoli (sacs) and destruction of some of the walls of the alveoli forming blebs. Chronic Obstructive Pulmonary Disease (COPD) is a chronic airway flow limitation and bronchitis that accompany emphysema in the elderly. Treatment: Oxygen therapy, inhaler that dilate the airway, steroid inhalers and surgical reduction of lung volume by resecting the blebs (air sacs or bubbles) in the lungs.

IV. Mesothelioma

It is a type of cancer that develops in the thin layer of tissue that covers the lung and the inside of the chest wall (pleura). It is most commonly found in these sites. However, it can occur in other sites covered by similar lining (called peritoneum), such as the stomach and intestine, the sack around the heart and rarely in the sack around the testicle. It is caused mostly by exposure to asbestos. The incidence in the elderly is increasing because of the longtime period between asbestos exposure and the development of the disease. It is a very lethal cancer despite its treatment with surgery, radiation therapy and chemotherapy.

V. Pulmonary Embolism

The diagnosis of this disorder in the elderly remains difficult and often missed due to the nonspecific and atypical presentation. The symptoms include dyspnea (shortness of breath), fast pulse, fast breathing, cough with occasional blood streaks and chest pain that gets worse with rest, while the pain of heart attacks feels better with rest. Arterial blood gases will reveal low oxygen concentration, electrocardiogram changes and chest X-ray will show an area in the periphery of lung without ventilation. A swollen leg (the site of blood clot) and chest pain can give a clue to the diagnosis of pulmonary embolism. Treatment: blood thinners, drugs to dissolve the clot and surgical removal of the clot called embolectomy.

VI. Pulmonary Hypertension

Pulmonary artery high blood pressure is the result of narrowing or blocking in the artery making it difficult for the blood to flow through the lung. It presents with shortness of breath, chest pain and fatigue. It will weaken the heart. Causes: parasitic infection, some drugs, genetic disorder, blood clots, lung tumors and pulmonary embolism. It cannot be cured, but management of symptoms can slow down the disease process. The management includes: the administration of blood vessel dilators to relax the vessels and reduce the pressure, drugs to prevent narrowing or constriction of vessels, enzymes to relax the pulmonary artery, calcium channel blocker to help heart muscle, blood thinners, digitalis (to strengthen the heart muscle) and drugs to help excretion of urine to reduce the load on the heart.

VII. Idiopathic Pulmonary fibrosis

It is a severe and chronic lung disease caused by fibrosis (scarring) of the lungs. This leads to respiratory failure and death. The median age at diagnosis is 66 years and the incidence increases with age. It starts with gradual shortness of breath and dry cough. As the disease progresses, the patient feels tired and develops clubbing of nails. The patient is liable to develop pulmonary hypertension, heart failure, pneumonia and pulmonary embolism. Causes: environmental pollution by inorganic dust such as silica and hard metal or by organic dust with animal protein.

There is no cure and the life expectancy is 3-5 years. Therapy: Oxygen therapy and lung transplant.

Sleep Disorders

1. Insomnia
2. Sleep Apnea
3. Restless Leg Syndrome

I. Insomnia

It is a disorder that interrupt daily life. The symptoms include:

1. Difficulty falling asleep at night and/or staying asleep.
2. Waking up at night and being unable to go back to sleep.
3. Waking up earlier than desired.
4. Feeling tired and unrefreshed in the morning.
5. This is accompanied by irritability, depression and anxiety,
6. Poor concentration and being uncoordinated.
7. Various gastrointestinal symptoms.
8. Worrying about sleep.

The causes could be physical or mental health issue. These include jet lag, job change, noise, high altitude, chronic pain, hormonal shift, high blood pressure, depression, stress, bipolar disorder and anxiety.

Treatment: sleeping medication, hormonal therapy, avoid heavy dinner before going to sleep, and avoid caffeine, nicotine and alcohol late at night.

II. Sleep Apnea

It is a very common disorder that occurs when the muscles in the back of the throat over relax. The symptoms are characterized by loud snoring followed by a period of stopped breathing. These symptoms are accompanied by restless sleeping, morning headache, feeling sleepy during the day, lack of energy, decreased interest in sex and insomnia.

Among the known causes of this disorder are overweight, enlarged tonsils and adenoids in the back of the throat, excessive alcohol consumption and smoking.

Treatment: 1. Continuous positive airway pressure.

2. Surgery on the uvula (end of soft palate).

III. Restless Leg Syndrome

It is a nervous disorder that causes an uncontrolled movement of the legs. It is caused by a sensation of crawling in the feet, calves and thighs with jerk movement of arms and legs. There are also feeling of tingling, burning, itching or throbbing and feeling of fizzy water in the blood vessels with cramping in calves, leg jerking, aching and itching. No known causes except for abnormalities in the brain with hereditary tendencies. It can be life long and no specific treatment available. However, it is recommended to increase dopamine level in the blood, the administration of calcium channel regulators, narcotic, sedatives and diet rich in iron.

Incontinence

t is the lack of voluntary control over urination or defecation. **Urinary Incontinence:** It is also called unintentional leakage of urine. It is caused by several factors that include: 1. excessive consumption of alcohol. 2. Medical conditions such as urinary tract infection, benign enlarged prostate, prostatic cancer, neurologic disorder, overactive urinary bladder, stress and urinary retention with an overflow. 3. Physical conditions such as pregnancy, child birth and aging.

Treatment: 1. drugs to decrease urinary bladder muscle spasm. 2. Drugs to make emptying the bladder easier. 3. Hormonal in females by tropical estrogen vaginal cream. 4. Bladder training with fluid and diet management. 5. Scheduled toilet trips. 6. Surgical procedure such as sling procedure, bladder neck suspension and surgery for uterine prolapse.

Bowel Incontinence: It is the inability to control bowel movement. It ranges from occasional leak while passing gas to complete loss of bowel control. It may be occasional during a bout of diarrhea or a sudden urge to defecate. It may be caused by chronic constipation and fecal impaction which can cause the anal and rectal muscles to stretch and get weak and leak.

Treatment: Nonsurgical preferred. An intake of 20-30 gm of fiber per day that makes stools bulky and easier to control. Avoid caffeine. Use daily laxatives to regulate bowel regimen. Drink a lot of water to avoid constipation. If no response, then proceed to further investigation to identify the cause in preparation for surgical approaches. These include: 1. anorectal measurement of the strength of the anal sphincter. 2. ultrasound to obtain images of the anal and rectal muscles.

3. Nerve tests to identify any nerve damage. The surgical procedures depend on the identified defect, and include sphincter surgery, sacral nerve stimulator, sphincter cuff surgery, and finally colostomy.

Urinary Tract Infection

t can affect the lower tract involving the urinary bladder and is called cystitis (bladder infection) which is the most common site of infection. On the other hand, when it affects the upper tract i.e. the kidney, it is called pyelitis. In the meantime, it can affect various sites of the tract such as urethra, prostate and the ureters.

The onset can be sudden and acute or repeatedly and chronic. The disease is more common in women because of the short urethra. It is usually caused by bacteria and rarely by virus. There are some contributing factors to getting urinary tract infections and these include: abnormally developed urological tract, medical conditions such as diabetes, stroke, spinal cord injury, weak immune system, pregnancy, menopause, kidney stones and the use of catheter in the urinary bladder.

The symptoms of cystitis include burning sensation during urination, frequent urination, pain and pressure in the lower abdomen, cloudy and smelly urine with occasional blood in the urine. The upper urinary tract infection (pyelitis) can present with fever, chills, back pain, nausea and vomiting.

The exact type of infection has to be identified by urinary examination (which include smear and culture and sensitivity). The treatment of upper and lower urinary tract infection is the same. Enforce fluid intake to flush the urinary system and use the proper antibiotics to counteract the infection. In addition, control back pain by local heat and narcotics, and lower abdominal pain by antispasmodic medications.

Osteoporosis

t is softening of the bones. It is caused by aging, lack of exercise, poor nutrition due to other disease conditions, chemotherapy for treatment of cancer, low calcium and vitamin D diet, smoking and excessive alcohol consumption. All these factors lead the bone to becomes brittle with stooped posture and frequent fractures mostly in hip, spine and wrist. This can be the first presenting symptom. However, if osteoporosis is suspected, bone density scan (DEXA) is performed as part of a physical examination.

Treatment: There is no cure. However, the treatment aims to slow down and hopefully to stop bone loss and improve bone density by medications. Prevent further bone loss by "Bisphosphonates", vitamin D, hormonal therapy; male hormone (such as testosterone) for men, and female hormone (estrogen) for women.

Falls in the Elderly

Falls are the main cause of injury and accidental death in people over 65 years of age. Falls can be a sign of poor health and declining function. More than 90% of hip fractures occur as a result of falls in persons over 70 years of age. Risk factors include increasing age, medications, cognitive disorders and sensory deficits. An elderly person who has fallen should be evaluated for the underlying cause and corrected to reduce the risk of repeated falls. The psychological impact of a fall or near fall can result in a fear of falling and increase self-restriction of activities leading to dependence and increasing immobility.

Prevention: It includes the modification of environmental hazards and the evaluation and treatment of blood pressure, vision problems and mental status changes including depression.

Interventions: Correct any of the possible disorders which may include postural hypotension, educate about appropriate use of sedatives, review of all medications, evaluate home safety as part of the evaluation of the environmental hazards, gait impairment, any impairment of balance and impairment of arms and legs strength. If needed, choose the correct aid; walker or wheelchair as the precautional measure.

Weight Loss in the Elderly

The common reasons for unintentional weight loss include depression, gastrointestinal disorders of various nature (including but not limited to gastroenteritis and chronic bowel diseases such as ileitis and Crohn's disease) and cancers. In addition, the aging process leads to changes which include loss of the lean body mass with decrease in muscle bulk. Elderly people eat less than they once did. This could be due to an increase in the hormone that causes a feeling of fullness and less hunger. Other causes include medical and nonmedical. Among the medical causes are viral infection by HIV (Human Immunodeficiency Virus), overactive thyroid and adrenal insufficiency. Psychological disorders including depression, reduced ability of smell and taste can reduce the appetite, and the decreased ability to chew reduces the rate of gastric emptying. Weight loss can be normal in nature or of no known causes.

Psychological
Disorders

Three common disorders occur in the elderly population. These include Anxiety, Depression and Delirium. While the early diagnosis can yield some beneficial therapy, the symptoms are sometimes ignored and blamed on aging until they become more advanced and harder to cure. In addition, some of the patients may have a combination of two of these disorders which may complicate the matter more. This may require a psychiatrist and a gastroenterologist to treat such disorder.

I. Anxiety

The earlier it is identified the easier it is to treat. However, the combination of depression and anxiety in the elderly is a more severe condition to treat and it usually follows severe trauma.

The symptoms include nervousness, restlessness, being tense, feeling of danger and pain. Panic attacks in the elderly present with trembling, heavy breathing, rapid heartbeat, rapid breathing, hyperventilation, chest pain and feeling of imminent death. The attack is short lived and not dangerous.

Treatment: 1. antianxiety medications that reduces abnormal electric activities in the brain. 2. Sedation.

II. Depression

As we grow older, we face significant life changes that increase the risk of depression. These include: 1. Health problems with disabilities, chronic aches and cognitive decline to the body image due to surgery or illness. 2. Social problems such as changes in residency, loss of finance, loss of independence, loneliness, loss of physical independence and emotional abuse. 3. Medical due to some medications.

The symptoms may include sadness, tiredness, trouble focusing or concentrating, unhappiness, anger, irritability, frustration, loss of interest, sleep problems, loss of energy and anxiety.

Treatment: Keep the patient talking, do not compare them to others, psychotherapy and medications including antidepressants and selective serotonin inhibitor.

III. Delirium

It is also known as "Acute Depression State" and is caused by a decline in the level of mental function. It varies in severity over a short period of time and includes attentional deficit and disorganization of behavior. Delirium occurs when the normal sending and receiving signals of the brain become impaired. It also may result from diseases unrelated to the brain such as urinary tract infection and pneumonia probably due to fever, certain medications, overconsumption of alcohol or drugs or sedatives withdrawal. Other predisposing factors include old age group over 65 years, men, dementia, depression, sensory impairment such as vision and hearing, dehydration and alcohol dependence. It may be difficult to diagnose.

Treatment: It is directed to control the underlying factors such as medications, alcohol consumption and infections.

Skin disorders

Skin diseases in the adults are usually due to life time sun exposure. As we age, the skin becomes thin and loses its elasticity due to collagen loss. As a result, it breaks easily, sags, get irritated easily and itches. The damage is more noticeable on the outer skin (on extensor site) than the inside skin (volar aspect) due to sun exposure.

Skin can be the site of inflammation, allergy, tumors benign and malignant. The most common tumor is Basal Cell Carcinoma which is locally invasive, treated by local excision or irradiation. However, its benign nature changes when the tumor reaches the mucosal surface (the lining of the mouth or nose) and becomes very aggressive. Melanoma is another serious tumor that is life threatening and requires the attention of a surgical oncologist, a radiotherapist and a medical oncologist. Sweat gland tumors are another dangerous group of tumors that need management by a surgical oncologist.

Gastrointestinal Disorders

Almost 40% of older adults have one or more related digestive symptoms. Some of these symptoms are related to aging, while others are not age related but could be from other causes. Example include: 1. Constipation which is due to slower moving intestinal contents due to aging, but it also can be induced by medications and inactivity such as pain medications and bed rest after a surgical procedure and poor intake of fluid. 2. Diverticulosis which is outpouching of the mucosa (lining of bowel) through the bowel wall. Causes are unknown. It can bleed or get inflamed causing bowel obstruction. 3. Bleeding from the stomach is common in the elderly population. It is induced by the use of Non-Steroidal Anti-Inflammatory Drugs (NSAIDs) that can cause stomach bleeding and ulcers which is not age related. 4. Difficulty swallowing food and fluids due to aging or due to disease such as dementia, stroke or Parkinson's disease. 5. Other findings that are common in old age groups is Gastro-Esophageal Reflux Disease (GERD) due to the reflux of the acid from stomach into the esophagus (common in old population and overweight individuals) causing uncomfortable burning sensation and needs the attention of the gastroenterologist and the surgeon. 6. Polyps (inside growth from the lining of the bowel) mostly in colon, and are of unknown causes, that need the attention of a gastroenterologist and a surgeon.

The Author Acknowledge Kara Elias and Joseph Elias
for their Reviewing and Editing the manuscript

Printed in the United States
By Bookmasters